Using Decimals to Plan Our Vacation

Andrew Einspruch

Real World Math Books are published by Capstone Press,
151 Good Counsel Drive, P.O. Box 669, Mankato, Minnesota 56002.
www.capstonepress.com

122009
005647WZS10

Library of Congress Cataloging-in-Publication Data
Einspruch, Andrew.
 Using decimals to plan our vacation / by Andrew Einspruch.
   p. cm. -- (Real world math)
 Includes index.
 ISBN 978-1-4296-5186-8 (library binding)
 1. Travel--Economic aspects--Juvenile literature. 2. Vacations--Economic aspects--Juvenile literature.
 3. Mathematics--Juvenile literature. I. Title. II. Series.

 G175.E48 2009
 513.5'5--dc22

2009051370

Editorial Credits
Sara Johnson, editor; Emily R. Smith, M.A.Ed., editorial director; Sharon Coan, M.S.Ed., editor-in-chief;
Lee Aucoin, creative director; Rachelle Cracchiolo, M.S.Ed., publisher

Photo Credits
The author and publisher would like to gratefully credit or acknowledge the following for permission
to reproduce copyright material: Cover Photolibrary.com; p.1 Photodisc; p.4 Getty Images/Phil Bankol;
p.5 (left and centre) Big Stock Photo; p.5 (right) Photolibrary.com/Alamy/Paul Crompton; p.6 (top left)
Photolibrary.com/Alamy/Jack Sullivan; p.6 (top right and bottom) Big Stock photo; p.7 iStock Photo;
p.8 (both) Big Stock Photo; p.9 Photolibrary.com/Alamy/David R. Frazier; p.10 (both) photodisc; p.11
photodisc; p.12 (left) Big Stock Photo; p.12 (right) Shutterstock; p.13 (top) 123RF; p13 (bottom)Getty
Images; p.14 Getty Images/Guy Bubb; p.15 Getty Images; p.16 Photolibrary.com/Alamy/Joanne O'Brien; p.17
(both) Big Stock Photo; p.18 (top) Getty Images/Dorling Kindersley; p.18 bottom Photos.com; p.19 Big
Stock Photo; p.20 Big Stock Photo; p.22 big Stock Photo; p.24 Photodisc; p.26-27 (both) Big Stock Photo;
p.28 Photolibrary.com/Alamy/Robert W. Ginn; p.29 Photolibrary.com/Alamy

While every care has been taken to trace and acknowledge copyright, the publishers tender their
apologies for any accidental infringement where copyright has proved untraceable. They would be
pleased to come to a suitable arrangement with the rightful owner in each case.

Table of Contents

To the Beach

Mom and Dad said we are going to the beach in 8 weeks for a vacation. Cool! There will be so much to do. My sister, Keandra, and I can't wait!

Mom has made a vacation **budget**. The budget is a plan that will help Mom and Dad figure out how much the vacation will cost. It will also help them figure out how much money to save to pay for it.

Money can be shown in **decimal** (DES-uh-muhl) form. A decimal point separates dollars and cents. Dollars are shown to the left of a decimal point. Cents are shown to the right.

There are 100 cents in a dollar. The numbers to the right of the decimal point show the part (or fraction) of 100 cents, or part of 1 dollar. The 2 place values after the decimal point are the tenths and hundredths places.

So, $1.15 = 1 dollar and 15 cents or 1 and 15 hundredths of a dollar.
$22.05 = 22 dollars and 5 cents or 22 and 5 hundredths of a dollar.
$100.00 = 100 dollars and no cents.

Hundreds	Tens	Ones	Decimal Point	Tenths	Hundredths
		1	.	1	5
	2	2	.	0	5
1	0	0	.	0	0

Draw a table like the one above. Then show:

a. $1.05   **b.** $78.40   **c.** $125.00

8 Weeks to Go

Mom showed me what she thinks things will cost. These are called our **expenses** (ex-PEN-suhz). They include money for gas and food. The beach house costs money, too. Mom also plans for fun stuff. She calls it **entertainment**.

The budget even has money for **unexpected** expenses. Mom says it's for "just in case!"

Our Vacation Expenses

Gas for car	$150.00
Beach house rental	$600.00
Food	$300.00
Unexpected expenses	$100.00

LET'S EXPLORE MATH

Look at the list of expenses above. Add up the money for vacation expenses listed. *Hint:* When you add decimals, always line up the decimal points one under the other.

Mom's giving Keandra and me $25.00 each! She says we can spend it on vacation. Mom says the whole vacation will cost $1,500.00.

Our Vacation Expenses

Gas for car	$150.00
Beach house rental	$600.00
Food	$300.00
Unexpected expenses	$100.00
Beach things (sunscreen, umbrella, beach towels, beach ball, beach chairs, beach bags, sunhats)	$200.00
Keandra's spending money	$25.00
Jimar's spending money	$25.00
Family entertainment	$100.00
Total	**$1,500.00**

Will We Have Enough Money?

Expenses are only part of Mom's budget. Saving money is also part of the budget. Mom and Dad have already saved $1,100.00.

Mom and Dad have their savings in the bank.

$1,500.00 expenses
− $1,100.00 savings
$ 400.00 still needed

Mom and Dad plan to save $50.00 per week between now and the vacation. The vacation is only 8 weeks away.

April

					1	2
3	4	5	6	7	$50	9
10	11	12	13	14	$50	16
17	18	19	20	21	$50	23
24	25	26	27	28	$50	30

May

1	2	3	4	5	$50	7
8	9	10	11	12	$50	14
15	16	17	18	19	$50	21
22	23	24	25	26	$50	28
29	30	31				

LET'S EXPLORE MATH

Mom and Dad are saving $50.00 for the next 8 weeks.

a. How much money will they save?

b. Draw the table below and write your answer in the correct columns.

Hundreds	Tens	Ones	Decimal Point	Tenths	Hundredths
			.		

What About Keandra and Me?

I will need more than $25.00 to pay for the things I want to do at the beach. Keandra thinks she will need more, too.

Mom told us to make a list of our vacation expenses. This will help us work out how much money we will need. We'll definitely need more money!

My (Jimar's) Vacation Expenses

Miniature golf $12.65
New goggles $7.35
Food and drinks $22.00
Movie ticket $9.00
DVD rental $5.50
Souvenirs $12.50

Keandra's Vacation Expenses

New swimsuit $30.00
New sandals $19.50
Food and drinks at the mall $27.95
Movie tickets (2 movies) $18.00
T-shirt $12.60
Sunglasses $20.75

LET'S EXPLORE MATH

Use Jimar's expenses above to answer the questions.

a. Work out the total amount Jimar will spend on "Food and drinks" and a "Movie ticket."

b. Order Jimar's expenses from the greatest amount to the least amount.

Keandra and I will have to make a budget! That way, we can plan how much money we will be able to save. First, we work out our **income**. I get $5.50 per week **allowance** (au-LAU-uhns). If I save it all for the next 8 weeks, and then add it to the $25.00 vacation spending money, how much will I have?

$5.50 per week

x   8 weeks to go
_____

= $44.00 savings

+ $25.00 from Mom and Dad
_____

= $69.00 total income

That is enough to cover my expenses!

Keandra has much more money than I do! She also gets $5.50 allowance. Then, she earns $15.75 per week babysitting. *And* she's already got $20.40 in savings.

Keandra's Income

$$\begin{aligned}
&\ \$15.75 \text{ earned at work} \\
+&\ \$5.50 \text{ allowance} \\
\hline
=&\ \$21.25 \text{ income each week} \\
\times&\ 8 \text{ weeks to go} \\
\hline
=&\ \$170.00 \text{ total income}
\end{aligned}$$

$$\begin{aligned}
&\ \$20.40 \text{ saved} \\
+&\ \$25.00 \text{ from Mom and Dad} \\
+&\ \$170.00 \text{ income} \\
\hline
=&\ \$215.40 \text{ spending money}
\end{aligned}$$

Keandra earns money from babysitting.

4 Weeks to Go

We have all been saving for our vacation. But yesterday our refrigerator broke! It was fixed, but it cost $400.00. This will come out of the vacation savings. Ouch!

<u>*Our Vacation Savings*</u>

$50.00 saved per week

x   4 weeks
_____

$200.00 saved

$1,100.00 already saved

+   200.00
_____

= $1,300.00 total savings

$1,300.00 saved

-      $400.00 repairs
_____

= $900.00 total savings

Mom and Dad's New Budget

Mom and Dad changed the budget to cover the cost of fixing the refrigerator. They will save $100.00 per week for the next 4 weeks.

Mom and Dad had to be clever to save extra money. They saved some money by looking out for **discounts** at the store.

SPECIAL OFFER

But, the vacation is supposed to cost $1,500.00! Mom and Dad are going to have to cut some vacation expenses. They will not be able to cut the cost of things like the beach house rental or the gas for the car. Which expenses can they cut?

LET'S EXPLORE MATH

Jimar's mom and dad will save $100.00 each week for the next 4 weeks. They have already saved $900.00 for the vacation.

a. What is the total amount of money they will save in the next 4 weeks?

b. Add this amount to the $900.00 they already saved. What will be the total amount saved?

Mom and Dad can save money in other ways. There will be less money for entertainment. We will not get new beach things, like beach towels or a beach ball.

And they are cutting my spending money! Keandra's too! We will now get $20.00 each.

Our Vacation Expenses

	Old Expenses	New Expenses
Gas for the car	$150.00	$150.00
Beach house rental	$600.00	$600.00
Food	$300.00	$275.00
Beach things (sunscreen, umbrella, beach chairs beach towels, beach ball, beach bags, sun hats)	$200.00	$100.00
Keandra and Jimar's spending money	$50.00	$40.00
Entertainment for the family	$100.00	$75.00
Unexpected expenses	$100.00	$60.00
Total	$1,500.00	$1,300.00

My New Budget

I got a library fine today! That means even less money to spend at the beach. I will have to change my budget.

My (Jimar's) New Vacation Budget
Income (Revised)

I planned to have $69.00 in income and $69.00 in expenses. That is $44.00 saved from my allowance, plus $25.00 from Mom and Dad.

But now I am only going to get $20.00 from Mom and Dad.

$44.00 savings
+ $20.00 from Mom and Dad
‾‾‾‾‾‾‾‾‾‾‾‾‾‾
= $64.00 to spend

And I have to subtract the money for my library fine.

$64.00 savings
− $5.00 library fine
‾‾‾‾‾‾‾‾‾‾‾‾‾‾
= $59.00 total income

So now I need to reduce my expenses.

	My (Jimar's) Old Expenses	My (Jimar's) New Expenses
Miniature golf	$12.65	$12.65
New goggles	$7.35	$7.35
Food and drinks	$22.00	$16.50
Movie ticket	$9.00	$9.00
DVD rental	$5.50	$5.50
Souvenirs	$12.50	$8.00
Total	$69.00	$59.00

I will not be able to do as many things as I planned. But at least I will **break even!**

LET'S EXPLORE MATH

Look at Jimar's *Old Expenses* and *New Expenses* above.

a. How much less money will Jimar spend on souvenirs?

b. How much less money will Jimar spend in total?

2 Weeks to Go

Keandra *thought* she had plenty of spare money. So she bought a dress for $65.00. But then she got sick. She missed 2 weeks of babysitting work! So she will lose $31.50 in pay! It is her turn to change her budget.

Keandra's Income (Revised)

$215.40 original spending money
− $5.00 less from Mom and Dad
− $65.00 dress
− $31.50 lost babysitting income
———————————————
 $113.90 total income

$65.00

Keandra's Vacation Expenses (Revised)

Old Expenses		New Expenses	
New swimsuit	$30.00	New swimsuit	$30.00
New sandals	$19.50	New sandals	$15.50
Food and drinks	$27.95	Food and drinks	$22.70
Movie tickets (2 movies)	$18.00	Movie ticket (1 movie)	$9.00
T-shirt	$12.60	T-shirt	$12.60
Sunglasses	$20.75	Sunglasses	$14.10
Old total	$128.80	**New total**	$103.90

Plus, Keandra will have $10.00 left for unexpected expenses.

LET'S EXPLORE MATH

Look at Keandra's *Old Expenses* and *New Expenses* above. How much less money will Keandra spend on:

a. food and drinks?

b. movie tickets?

c. sunglasses?

1 Week to Go

We just found out the beach has **scuba diving** lessons! Keandra and I have to try that! The lessons cost $20.00. So we need to change our budgets again.

Keandra has $10.00 for unexpected expenses. She can put that toward the scuba lessons. But we both still need to save money by cutting our expenses once more.

My (Jimar's) Budget
Total Income: $59.00

	Old Expenses	New Expenses
Miniature golf	$12.65	$12.65
~~New goggles~~	~~$7.35~~	$0.00
Food and drinks	$16.50	$12.35
Movie ticket	$9.00	$9.00
~~DVD rental~~	~~$5.50~~	$0.00
Souvenirs	$8.00	$5.00
Scuba lessons	——	$20.00
Total	$59.00	$59.00

Keandra's Budget
Total Income: $113.90

	Old Expenses	New Expenses
New swimsuit	$30.00	$28.00
New sandals	$15.50	$10.50
Food and drinks	$22.70	$19.70
Movie ticket (1 movie)	$9.00	$9.00
T-shirt	$12.60	$12.60
Sunglasses	$14.10	$14.10
~~Unexpected expenses~~	~~$10.00~~	$0.00
Scuba lessons	——	$20.00
Total	$113.90	$113.90

Vacation Time!

Waves and sun, here we come! Mom and Dad saved $1,300.00, and Keandra and I have our money, too. It's going to be a great week! Now, do I play mini golf first or take scuba lessons?

LET'S EXPLORE MATH

Jimar's family is finally on vacation. How much money did the family save in total for their trip? *Hint:* Make sure you look at Jimar and Keandra's final budgets on page 25, and Mom and Dad's budget on page 19.

Hot Dog Heaven

Chris plays on a local basketball team. The team needs new uniforms, but the club does not have any money. New uniforms cost $5.00 each. Chris wants to help in any way he can. He has decided to raise some money by setting up a hot dog stand at his school fair. He wants to sell 100 hot dogs. He works out the cost of the ingredients. These are his expenses.

50 hot dogs = $100.00

50 hot dog buns = $25.00

4 bottles of ketchup = $14.00

4 jars of mustard = $16.00

Solve It!

a. If Chris sells all 100 hot dogs for $3.50 each, how much money will he earn? This is his income.

b. How much money did Chris make after paying for his expenses? This is his profit.

c. How many uniforms will the club be able to buy?

Use the steps below to help you solve the problems.

Step 1: Find the cost of 100 hot dogs, 100 hot dog buns, 8 bottles of ketchup, and 8 jars of mustard.
Hint: Double the costs listed on page 28.

Step 2: Add up all the expenses.

Step 3: Find the income from the sale of 100 hot dogs.

Step 4: Subtract the cost of expenses from the income from the sales. The money left over is the profit. Chris can use the profit to buy the uniforms.

Step 5: Divide the profit by $5.00.

Glossary

allowance—a fixed amount of pocket money

break even—being able to spend as much money as you earn, and no more

budget—a plan to work out how much money you earn and spend over a period of time

decimal—a number based on 10

discounts—sale prices that are lower than the original amounts of items

entertainment—things that people do for fun, not for work

expenses—things that people spend money on

income—an amount of money earned

scuba diving—underwater swimming done with a portable air tank

unexpected—not predicted or planned for

Index

Internet Sites

FactHound offers a safe, fun way to find Internet sites related to this book. All of the sites on FactHound have been researched by our staff.

Here's all you do:

Visit *www.facthound.com*

FactHound will fetch the best sites for you!

ANSWER KEY

Let's Explore Math

Page 5:

Hundreds	Tens	Ones	Decimal Point	Tenths	Hundredths
		1	.	0	5
	7	8	.	4	0
1	2	5	.	0	0

Page 7:
$1,150.00

Page 10:
a. Mom and Dad will save $400.00
b.

Hundreds	Tens	Ones	Decimal Point	Tenths	Hundredths
4	0	0	.	0	0

Page 12:
a. Food and drinks $22.00
    + Movie ticket $9.00
    Total $31.00
b. My (Jimar's) Vacation Expenses
    Food and drinks $22.00
    Miniature golf $12.65
    Souvenirs $12.50
    Movie ticket $9.00
    New goggles $7.35
    DVD rental $5.50

Page 17:
a. $100.00 x 4 weeks = $400.00
b. $400.00 + $900.00 = $1,300.00 saved

Page 21:
a. Jimar will spend $4.50 less on souvenirs.
    ($12.50 – $8.00 = $4.50)
b. Jimar will spend $10.00 less in total.
    ($69.00 – $59.00 = $10.00)

Page 23:
a. Keandra will spend $5.25 less on food and drinks. ($27.95 – $22.70 = $5.25)
b. Keandra will spend $9.00 less on movie tickets. ($18.00 – $9.00 = $9.00)
c. Keandra will spend $6.65 less on sunglasses. ($20.75 – $14.10 = $6.65)

Page 26:
Jimar's family saved a total of $1,472.90.
($1,300.00 + $59.00 + $113.90 = $1,472.90)

Problem-Solving Activity

50 hot dogs = $100.00. So 100 hot dogs:
$100.00 × 2 = $200.00
50 hot dog buns = $25.00. So 100 hot dog buns: $25.00 × 2 = $50.00
8 bottles of ketchup = $28.00
8 jars of mustard = $32.00

Expenses
        $200.00
         $50.00
         $28.00
         $32.00
Total: $310.00

a. Chris will earn $350.00
b. $350.00 income – $310.00 expenses = $40.00 profit
c. The club will be able to buy 8 uniforms.
    $40.00 profit ÷ $5.00 cost of uniform = 8 uniforms